ON THE ROAD

FIRST EDITION COLLECTION

This book is dedicated to all our family and friends who have believed in us from the very beginning. In particular, we would like to thank Judy Boychuk Duchscher, sister of Brian and Ron, who was, and continues to be, a pillar of overwhelming support, spirit and infectious enthusiasm. Special mention also goes to Kevin Blevins of the Leader-Post in Regina, who recognized our potential early on and gave us our first big break. Last but not least, we would like to thank our wives for putting up with our endless phone calls and our unwavering belief that through total commitment and sheer determination, dreams can come true.

CHUCKLE BROS

ON THE ROAD
FIRST EDITION COLLECTION

by

Brian Boychuk
Ron Boychuk
Ronnie Martin

CREATIVE
DESIGNS

Chuckle Bros is not currently syndicated.

First printing, December 2005

Printed on recycled paper.

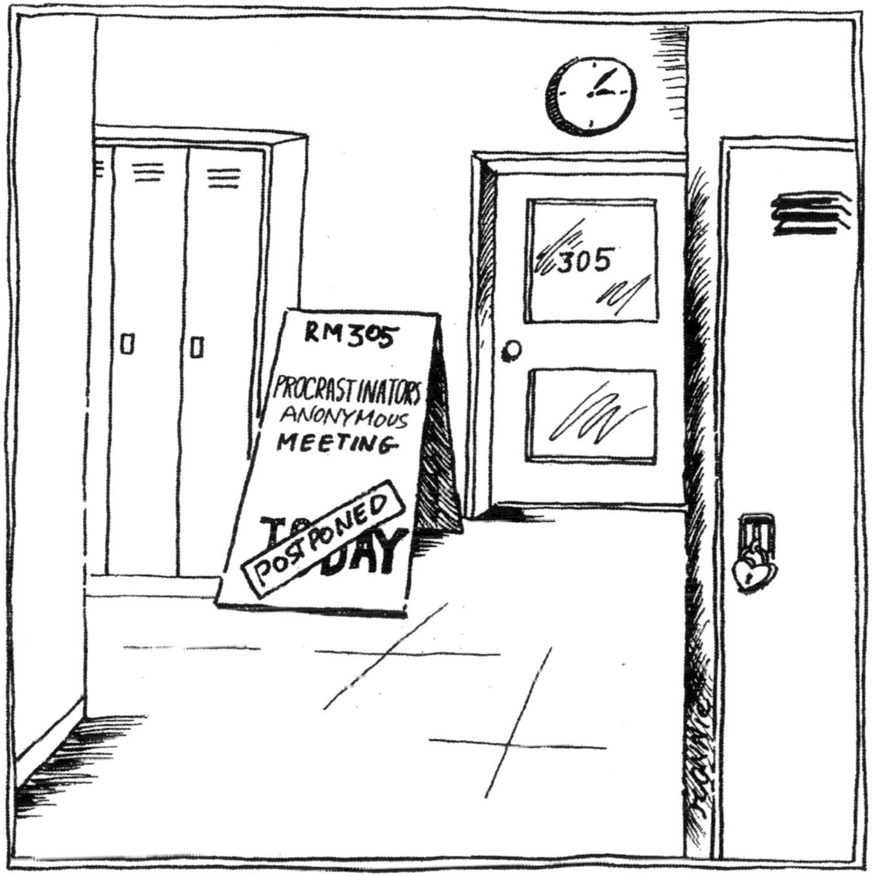
RM 305
PROCRASTINATORS
ANONYMOUS
MEETING
POSTPONED
DAY
305

Evelus Knievelus

Satellite pirates of the Caribbean

" . . . and you expect the court to believe that my client
'accidentally' fell on his sword? Surely you jest."

The Kindersley brothers return from yet another
successful crap shoot.

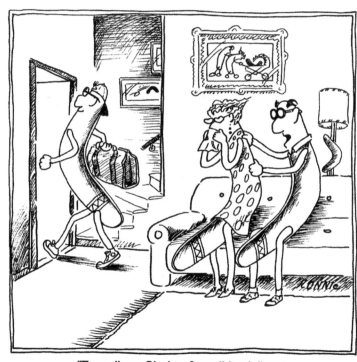

"There, there Gladys. Something tells me
he'll be right back."

"T minus 10 . . 9 . . 8 . . . 7 . . . . 5 . . . . er . . 2 . . . . uh . . . . . . 6.
Dang! I hate counting backwards."

"Well, Mike, you got me there.
Perhaps I didn't make myself perfectly clear."

9

"As you can clearly see, Kevin, we're going to have to let you go."

Medieval pranksters

"Hold the door, Dr. Johnston! I'll just get my purse."

12

Carl was relieved to hear that it was only his nights that were numbered, not his days.

"Well, Pat, this should be an interesting matchup. Not since Ali have we seen opponents with these particular skills."

"Good Lord, Baskins! This creature, if it really does exist,
could probably carry off a man."

Curse of the Mummy

Just another day at the Bermuda International Airport.

"We've had reports that someone in the tournament is sandbagging. You gentlemen know anything about this?"

15

"Hold on a second, Dave. It says here it's a 'retinal' scanner."

"O.K. Dwayne, why don't you start us off."

"Well, for Pete's sake. That's the third display this week.
I don't understand it."

Gerry's internal clock told him it was time to get up.
Unfortunately, it was about 127 years too fast.

"What in tarnation do you think you're doing?
The show's over there!"

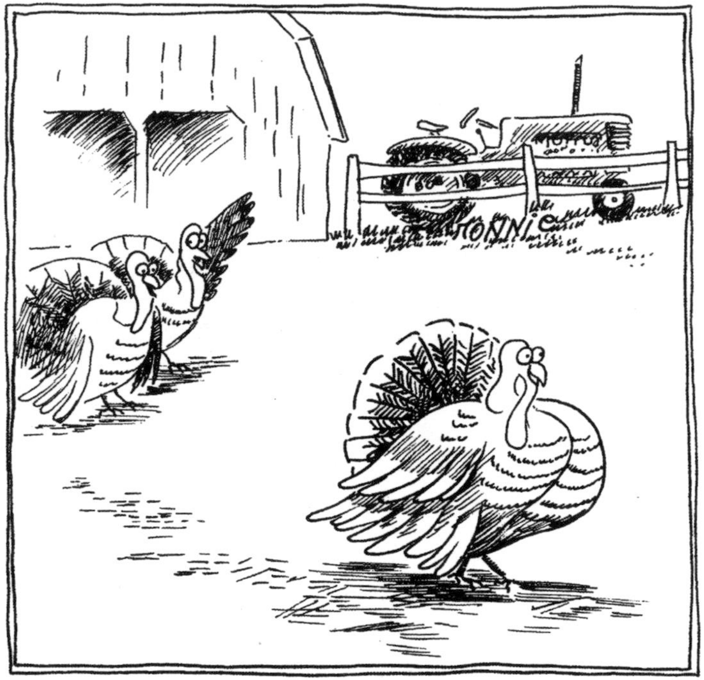

"Implants."

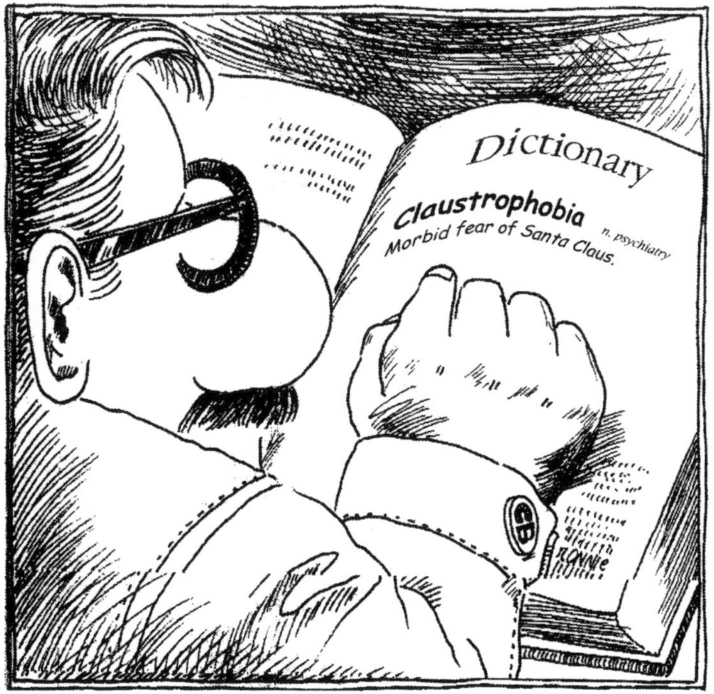
Dictionary
Claustrophobia
n. psychiatry
Morbid fear of Santa Claus.

Rejected Olympic Demonstration Sports
The 100 Meter Indoor 8-Man Scull

Monkey bars

"They have a good two days' head start on us boys,
so let's move out . . . and Parker, try to keep up this time."

"I still think this is a complete waste of time."

Napoleon's first and only attempt at large scale oils.

To this day, Larry cannot for the life of him figure out
how he got so separated from the pack.

When an editor inadvertently flips a cartoon.

25

"Of course you can go outside and play with Daddy.
Just make sure you're not dressed too warmly."

"Ya know, Jake? Sometimes I can't tell whether
I'm a'comin or a'goin."

"Sorry, Elliott. I didn't see your plane there."

How yodelling got started

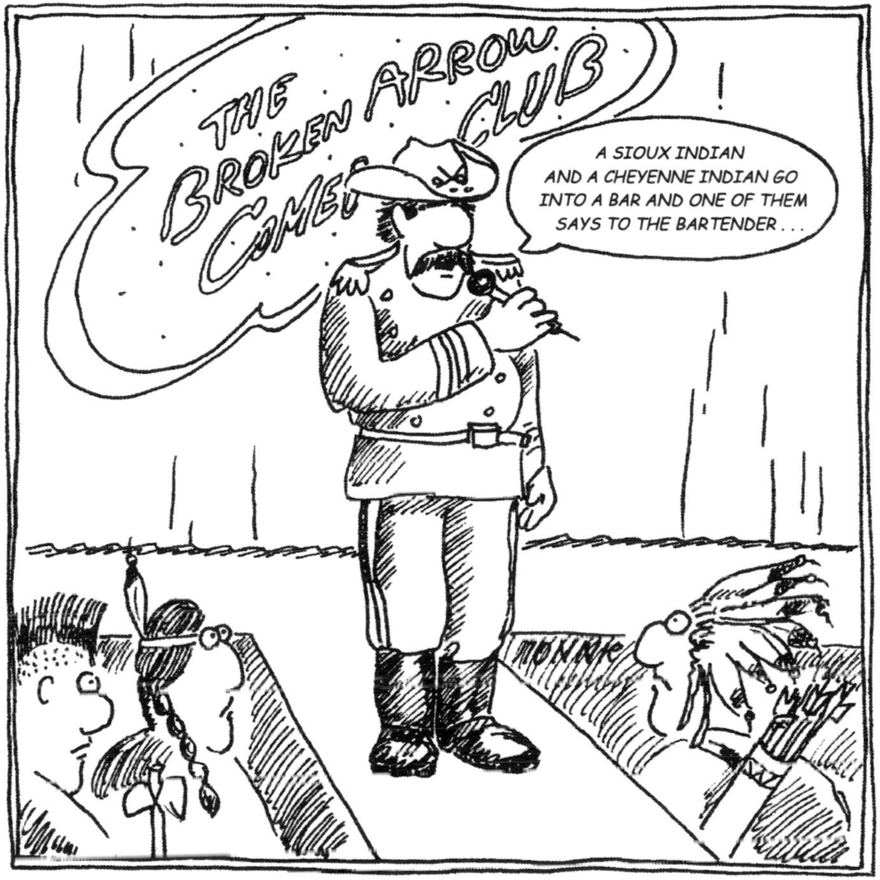
THE BROKEN ARROW
CLUB
A SIOUX INDIAN AND A CHEYENNE INDIAN GO INTO A BAR AND ONE OF THEM SAYS TO THE BARTENDER . . .

Custer's last stand-up

Where aliens go to hone their skills.

Orville never really understood why his pa insisted
he get his ducks cleaned every three years.

Orchestral percussion instruments: the Brazilian woodblock,
the Peruvian cowbell and the Bermuda triangle

Unfortunately for volunteer technician Karl Jacuzzi, he was never to know how synonymous his name would become with whirlpool jet tubs.

"You're right Dick, that's one terrific Riverdance number, but whatever happened to just spiking the ball?"

"Whooowee! That's quite the hair trigger there, eh Billy?"

"What the . . ."

"Oooohh, Harold! They're my favorite. How did you know?"

It was shortly after this incident that track pants were made mandatory at all gymnastic events.

"You're right, Ralph, this IS a long light."

"This must be where the rubber met the road."

"Would an aircraft mechanic please report to the baggage claim area."

Cartoon talk balloon vendors.

"Boy, there sure are a lot of no-shows."

"We hear there was a lightning strike in your area.
Any word on that, Bill?"

"Sure it's a bit pricey, but you know what they say -
location, location, location."

"Team number one, we're going to need an answer."

"I'm sorry, Frank, but I just can't see you any more."

Christmas at the home of drag racing legend
"Big Daddy" Don Garlitts.

"I remember when this was farm land
for as far as the eye could see."

A typical home of the travelling salesman.

45

"I hear they sell a ton of neat stuff in here."

Just another annoying vacuum salesman

"Sure, he's a good player, but yesterday
I cleaned his clock."

"I think I found the reason your computer is running so slow."

Living up to its name, the "SpineBuster" was quietly dismantled after its inaugural run and never spoken of again.

"I gotta hand it to ya, boss. Escaping on Independence Day was a stroke of genius."

**Rejected Olympic Demonstration Sports
Four Man Sumo Bobsledding**

The Cymbal Indians return from yet
another unsuccessful hunt.

"Just wait until he finds the range."

"How many times do I have to tell you to PLAY with your food?"

**Rejected Olympic Demonstration Sports
The Very High Bar**

54

"Pardon me sir, would you happen to have a compass for a
1972 Delta-class nuclear-powered ballistic missile submarine?"

In an effort to prove his father wrong, Dr. Peterson,
Head of Horticulture, tends to his money trees.

"Technically, he shouldn't be able to do it, Wally, but he
does. You know? I mean, he always
seems to get us there O.K."

Armchair quarterbacks

"Be careful with that one, it was a wedding gift."

"Man, that guy's good."

The Great Manfredini goes out in a blaze of glory.

60

"Trust me, Count. You look terrific!"

"Well, that's it for this week Mr. Farnsworth. We've tried just about everything to get rid of your erratic tee shots, but nothing seems to work."

"Dang! He must have just stepped out . . . again!"

"You're new at this, aren't you Dad?"

65

"Come on, Sparky! Atta boy! Just a weeeee bit higher."

The legendary Serengeti film crew in action.

"Ha! Looks like I got the last cup. I guess
you're outta luck, Jerry."

"Honestly, Zoltar, I could have sworn I parked it right here."

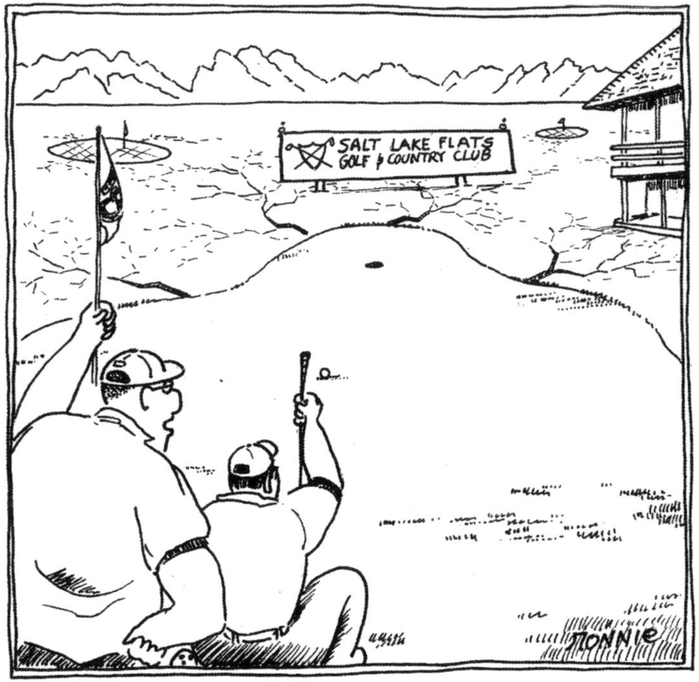
SALT LAKE FLATS
GOLF & COUNTRY CLUB
RONNIE

"Well I'll be, Mike. This one is absolutely straight in too."

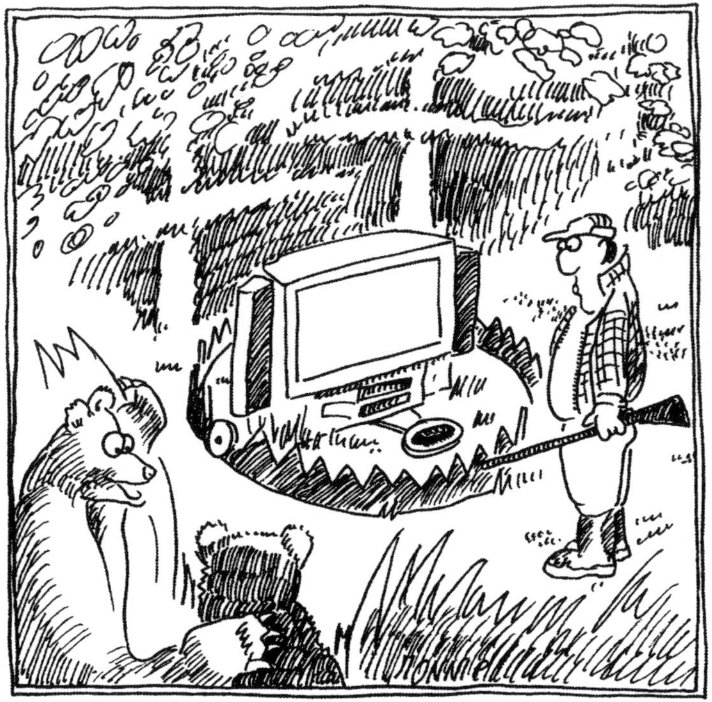

"Watch and learn, son."

Part I in the "Where Are They Now?" series.

"What do you mean you've been sent? What are you, wise guys?"

"Oh, hi Ron. You know Brian and his projects. He's probably
painted himself into a corner as we speak.
Just a minute, I'll get him."

Rejected Olympic Demonstration Sports
The 200 Meter Pole Vault Dash

"All right, you've had your fun.
Now get out there and knock the stuffing out of him!"

What medieval executioners do on a slow day.

A Venetian SUV

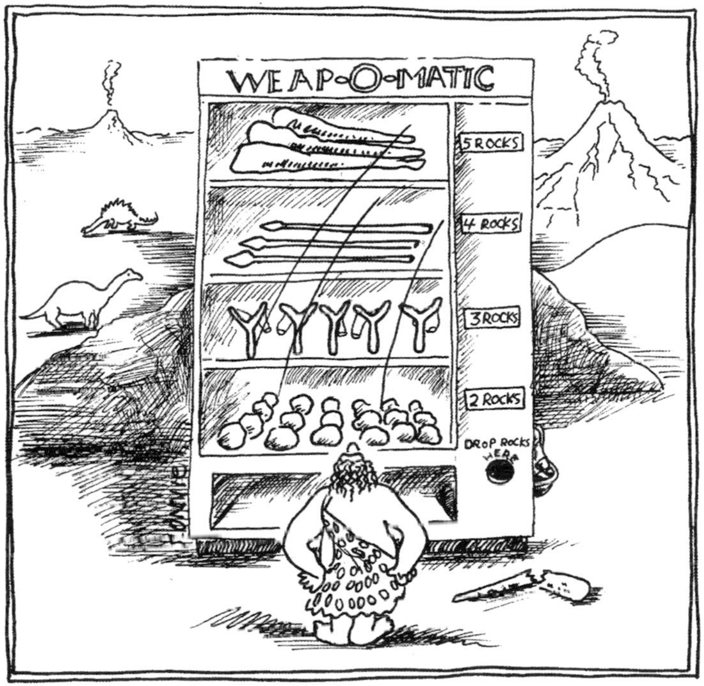
WEAP-O-MATIC
5 ROCKS
4 ROCKS
3 ROCKS
2 ROCKS
DROP ROCKS HERE

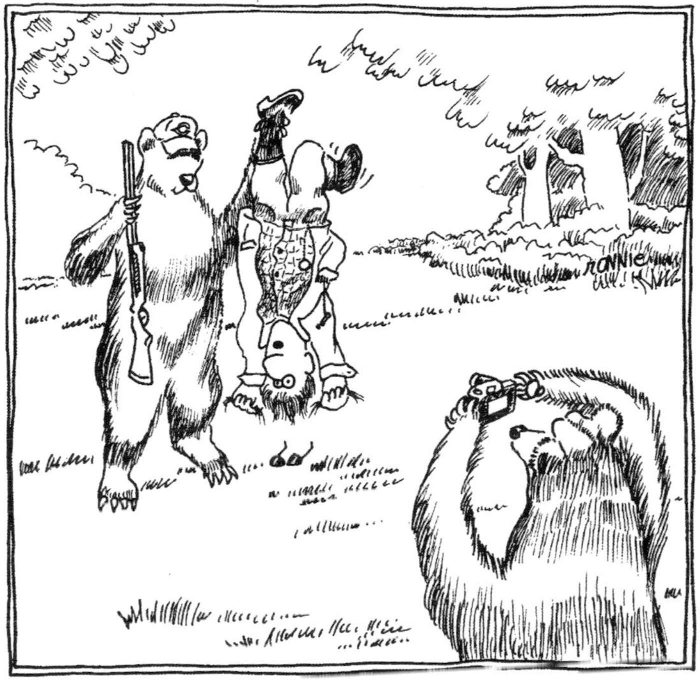

A Kodiak moment

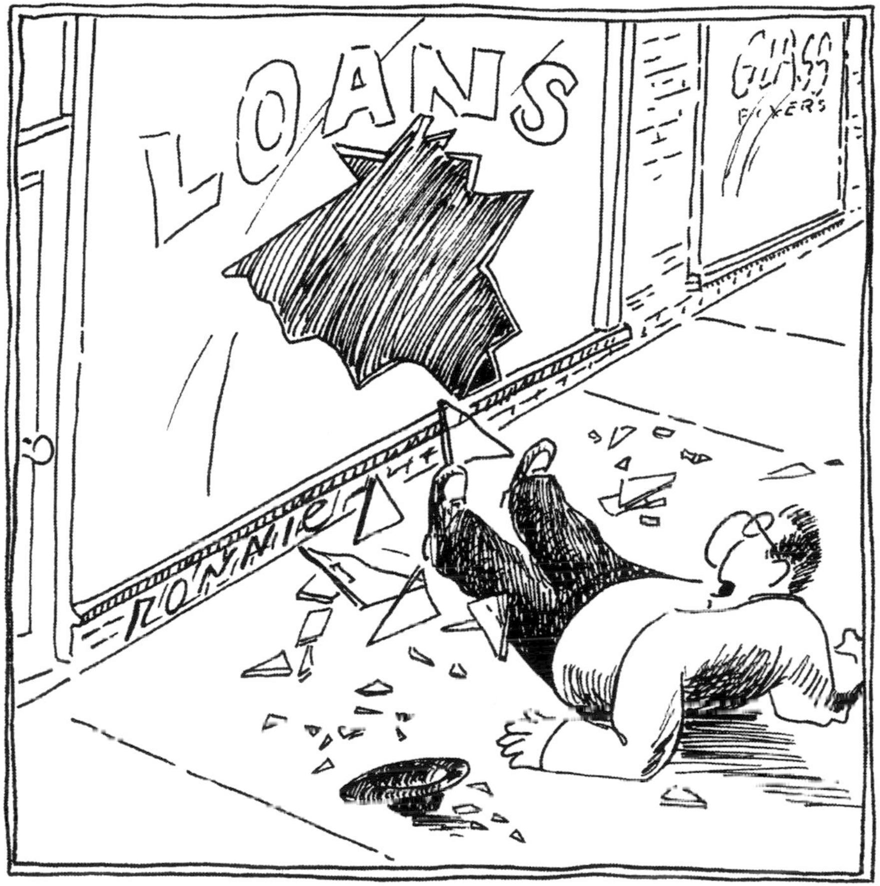
LOANS
GLASS
FIXERS
RONNIE

"I take it that's a 'no'."

"Thank you all for coming and may I say how wonderful it is to see such a full house tonight!"

"Would you like me to supersize that?"

We at the Chuckle Bros hope you found our
brand-new single-panel cartoon enjoyable.

Please feel free to let us know
what you thought by visiting us at
chucklebros.com
and leaving us an email.

Your comments would be greatly appreciated.